The canyon was sizzling hot and dry as dust. . . .

Rattlesnakes rested in the shade of every juniper bush. It was perfect dinosaur-hunting country!

Barnum Brown and his team walked along the ridges and in the deep gullies. A tiny piece of fossil bone could be the clue that led them to a giant.

Way up on the side of a rocky slope, Brown saw large bones sticking out of the sand. He brushed the soft sand away to get a better look. Soon he hit hard rock.

In the rock were bones of a huge meat-eating dinosaur.

The most exciting, most inspiring,
most unbelievable stories . . .
are the ones that really happened!

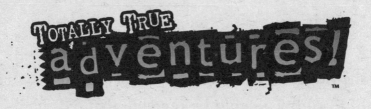

The $25,000 Flight

Babe Ruth and the Baseball Curse

Balto and the Great Race

The Curse of King Tut's Mummy

Finding the First T. Rex

The Titanic *Sinks!*

TOTALLY TRUE adventures!

FINDING THE FIRST
T. REX

by Kathleen Weidner Zoehfeld

illustrated by Jim Nelson

A STEPPING STONE BOOK™

Random House 🏠 New York

For Dr. Bob, Capt. James Kipp,
and the Big Paddlefish
—K.W.Z.

For my mom
—J.N.

Text copyright © 2008 by Kathleen Weidner Zoehfeld
Interior illustrations copyright © 2008 by Jim Nelson
Photograph credits: pg. 101 © astrangerinthealps, some rights reserved. pg. 102:
(top) © mrkathika, some rights reserved; (bottom) © Gary Burke, all rights
reserved. pg. 103 courtesy of the Library of Congress. pg. 104: (top) © lebovox,
all rights reserved; (bottom) © aaron gustafson, some rights reserved. pg. 105 ©
paul heaston, all rights reserved.

Visit us on the Web!
SteppingStonesBooks.com
randomhouse.com/kids

Educators and librarians, for a variety of teaching tools, visit us at
RHTeachersLibrarians.com

Library of Congress Cataloging-in-Publication Data
Zoehfeld, Kathleen Weidner.
Finding the first T. rex / by Kathleen Weidner Zoehfeld ;
illustrated by Jim Nelson.
    p. cm.
"A Stepping Stone Book."
ISBN 978-0-375-84662-5 (pbk.) — ISBN 978-0-375-94662-2 (lib. bdg.)
1. Tyrannosaurus rex—Juvenile literature. I. Nelson, Jim, ill. II. Title.
QE862.S3Z63 2008   567.912'9—dc22   2007027730

Printed in the United States of America   10 9 8 7 6

This book has been officially leveled by using the F&P Text Level Gradient™
Leveling System.

Contents

Life and Death,
Long, Long Ago

Sixty-seven million years ago, two giant meat-eaters battled. They shoved each other with their big, knobby heads. They opened their horrible jaws. And they snapped their saw-edged teeth. Their thumps, chomps, and grunts rang through the steamy swamp where they lived.

Finally one of the monsters fell to the

ground. His wounds were bad. After a few minutes, he died.

This was nothing new. Fights like this one had gone on every day for millions of years. And they would happen day after day for millions of years to come.

Animals are born and animals die. Most of the time, they leave no record of their lives. But this dead giant was lucky. Soon after his death, a nearby river flooded. It covered his bones with a thick blanket of sand. Safe under the sand, his bones became fossils. They lay underground—waiting. . . .

1

A Museum in
Need of a Monster

In 1876, America celebrated its one hundredth birthday. The Civil War was over. And the country was growing. The wild land where dinosaurs once battled had changed. The steamy swamps were long gone. Now everything was dry. Instead of dinosaurs, wolves and bison lived there. The area was known as the Montana Territory. Pioneers were moving west. They were building new homes and ranches.

Back east, big buildings were going up everywhere. On June 2, 1874, the president of the United States, Ulysses S. Grant, made a special trip to New York City. On that day, he laid the first stone

for a new museum. It would become the American Museum of Natural History.

Two years later, the museum was almost done. Across the street, Central Park had just opened. People came to enjoy the new park. While they were there, they could watch the museum taking shape.

The six-story brownstone building with arched windows stood in the middle of a large, empty lot. Uptown was still pretty rustic at that time. Goats frisked on the grounds. They drank from the muddy puddles and grazed on the weeds.

Finally, on December 22, 1877, the last of the stray goats had been rounded up, and everything was ready for opening day. A crowd of excited New Yorkers waited for a tour of their new museum. Once inside they were in for a treat.

The museum was brimming with weird and wonderful things! It had the bones of an extinct dodo. A mastodon tooth. A camel from Armenia. Wild buffalo from the forests of Lithuania. A moose from Nova Scotia. A wapiti from the Rocky Mountains. And dozens of stuffed rats and mice.

Each item was carefully labeled. Smaller items were locked in glass cases. People stared in awe at 3,000 colorful birds, 4,000 beetles, 4,000 seashells, sixteen types of algae, and thousands of fossil clams and snails.

But this was only the beginning. The museum's founder, Albert Bickmore, saw a great future for the museum. He planned to make the collections even bigger. He wanted to add new wings to the building. Before long, the American Museum of Natural History would be the biggest and best natural history museum in the world. Millions of people would come to New York just to see it.

New Yorkers were proud of the new museum. But after the first few weeks, they began to get bored. After a few months, hardly anyone visited. Day after day, Bickmore and his staff paced the lonely halls. Money was running out.

By 1880, the museum's directors were very worried. One of them, Morris Jesup, was a self-made millionaire. The directors asked him to be president of the museum. He was good with money. Maybe he could help.

Jesup studied the problem. To him, it seemed hopeless. Not enough people were interested in the museum's collections. It was as simple as that. He said the museum had to close.

But Bickmore wouldn't let go of his dream. He walked through the museum with Jesup. He pointed out each clam and snail. And he explained how rare and important they were. These fossils could

help scientists tell the age of the earth itself. They could help unlock the secrets of how life evolved.

When he was a kid, Jesup liked school. But he had to quit after sixth grade. His father died. And at the age of twelve, Jesup had to work to support his family.

Now—right there in the museum—he was getting the education he had always wanted. It was even more interesting than he had imagined. He changed his mind about the museum. No matter what it cost, it must stay open. The people of New York needed this place. He just had to get them as excited about it as he was.

Instead of closing, he told the directors the museum had to grow even bigger. They asked how the museum would pay for more treasures. And where would they keep them all? Jesup told them not to worry. He'd figure it out.

For the next ten years, Jesup helped every part of the museum grow. Just as Bickmore dreamed, new wings were added. But where were the crowds? People were still not flocking to the great museum.

Jesup noticed that crowds *were* flocking to the Academy of Natural Sciences in Philadelphia. Why? Because they had a big dinosaur skeleton from New Jersey!

The first dinosaur displays went up in England in the 1820s. Since then, people had gone dinosaur-crazy. In America, the famous bone hunters Edward Drinker Cope and Othniel Charles Marsh were making headlines in all the big newspapers. The two men found many huge dinosaur skeletons in Colorado and Wyoming. They shipped the bones back east. People couldn't wait to get a look at them.

The American Museum of Natural History didn't have any dinosaurs. Jesup dreamed of putting up a huge dinosaur skeleton in his museum. Then the crowds would come! Once people were there, they would see how great the whole collection was—snails, clams, dinosaurs, and all!

2

Wanted: Talented
Bone Hunter

In 1891, Jesup hired Henry Fairfield Osborn, a tall, handsome professor from Princeton University. His job would be to find fossil bones for the museum. Jesup didn't ask Osborn to look for dinosaurs right away. He knew the young man was more interested in fossil mammals.

While Osborn was collecting mammals,

another museum opened. This one was in Pittsburgh, Pennsylvania. The founder was a millionaire named Andrew Carnegie. He wanted his museum to be bigger and more important than the American Museum of Natural History. Suddenly Osborn had a rival.

So far, the American Museum of Natural History had only two big mammal skeletons on display. One was a mastodon. The other was a giant Irish elk.

The new Carnegie Museum of Natural History put a mastodon and a giant Irish elk on display, too.

Osborn figured it wouldn't be long before Carnegie found something even bigger. He'd have to get his hands on more skeletons. And he'd have to do it fast. If he took much longer, people might forget all about the natural history museum in New York City!

Jesup told Osborn to buy some fossils from Edward Drinker Cope. But what Jesup and Osborn really wanted was to send crews out on big bone-hunting trips. They needed eager young scientists with sharp eyes for finding fossils.

In 1897, Osborn met a young man from Kansas named Barnum Brown. Barnum did not seem like a very good name for a scientist. (At that time, everyone had heard of P. T. Barnum. He was the founder of the world's most famous circus.) But Brown's name had a good story behind it. On the day he was born, the circus was in town. His older brother and sister loved it so much, they asked their parents to name the new baby Barnum.

In spite of the flashy name, Osborn liked the young man. Barnum had grown up on a farm in America's heartland. From the time he was old enough to walk, he had looked for fossils. To earn extra money, Barnum's father did some coal-mining. While he ran the coal plow, Barnum followed behind. He studied the stones that were turned up. Sometimes those stones had fossil shells in them.

Barnum asked a lot of questions. Why did he find shells in the middle of Kansas? He had never even seen the ocean. Yet he filled his pockets with fossil corals and seashells almost every day.

Barnum kept them in the dresser in his bedroom. Soon the drawers were overflowing. His mother made him move the fossils to the laundry shed in the backyard.

There Barnum started his first museum.

He read about the ancient oceans that once covered most of the Midwest. Millions of years ago, no wheat or sunflowers grew in Kansas. Instead, a gray-blue ocean stretched out as far as the eye could see. It was filled with strange fish and sharp-toothed sea reptiles.

As a college student, Brown took fossil-collecting trips to Nebraska, South Dakota, and Wyoming. He went with his professor and a group of other students. For weeks at a time, they camped in places far from cities or towns.

Brown was a great help on those trips. He looked after the horses and made sure everyone was well fed. He took care of the wagons. And he kept all the tools in good order. Brown had many talents, but one was most important. He seemed to be able to sniff out fossils, no matter where he went.

In the summer of 1897, Osborn asked Barnum Brown to search for fossils for the American Museum of Natural History. He sent Brown to Como Bluff, Wyoming. Cope and Marsh had found some of their biggest dinosaurs there. Osborn didn't know if they'd find any more dinosaurs at Como Bluff. He was pretty sure there would be some ancient mammals, though. So he wanted to have a look.

Brown searched the bare, rocky out-crops for weeks. He had no luck at all. A few weeks later, Osborn joined Brown and the crew in Wyoming.

As soon as Osborn got there, Brown's luck turned. He found a fossil graveyard full of hundreds of big bones. Brown couldn't wait to start digging. Later that year, Osborn described the find to everyone back home. Some of those bones, he said, were from a "reptile of magnificent size." The American Museum of Natural History had bagged its first dinosaur!

3

Triceratops Hunt

The new dinosaur was a huge, long-necked, plant-eating *Diplodocus*. Finding it made Jesup and the museum's directors very happy. But trouble was brewing for Osborn. In Pittsburgh, Andrew Carnegie read the news about Brown's "reptile of magnificent size" and others like it. The stories set his imagination on fire. He wanted a big dinosaur for his museum, too. In 1899, he met with two of Osborn's best workers. He talked them into coming to work for him.

Carnegie gave them maps and tools and sent them straight to Wyoming. After a few weeks, they had found two *Diplodocuses*—the front end of one and the

rear end of another. Put together, the two skeletons made one nearly perfect dinosaur. They named him "Dippy." Dippy's skeleton was much more complete than the one Brown found.

Osborn was steamed, but he had a secret. That very summer, one of his crews was busy uncovering another dinosaur. It was a little shorter than Dippy, but it was much heavier. It was a seventy-foot-long, plant-eating *Apatosaurus*.

Osborn knew it would be a few years before they could get the huge skeleton on display. But once that *Apatosaurus* was all put together and up, the American Museum of Natural History would be able to brag. It would be the home of the biggest, heaviest, most complete dinosaur mounted anywhere.

Meanwhile, they put up a "mammoth sea lizard" and two of the smaller dinosaurs from the Como Bluff area. By 1900, things were looking pretty good for New York's natural history museum. Even though the big *Apatosaurus* wasn't ready yet, visitors began to come by the thousands.

The museum's crews took photos of the sunbaked gullies where they worked. Osborn had the photos blown up. He hung them on the museum walls near the bones. For the first time, visitors could see where the bone hunters spent their summers. It was easy to tell why those places were called "badlands." The people wanted more. More photos! And more bones!

Osborn met with his star dinosaur hunter, Barnum Brown. He told him there was one important dinosaur they needed now—a *Triceratops*.

Triceratops bones had been found years ago in Wyoming. The Smithsonian, in Washington, D.C., would soon be ready to display the first whole skeleton. It was twenty feet long and over eight feet high. Osborn knew the three-horned monster would be a big hit.

That June, Osborn sent Brown back to Wyoming. Brown and his crew didn't find much. They returned to New York with only a few *Triceratops* bones, some fossil leaves, and a fossil turtle. But there was something else. Osborn found it very interesting. Brown had dug up a jaw full of huge teeth!

Brown and Osborn brushed the dirt away from the big jaw. They stared at it in

awe. The teeth were as thick as bananas. They were six inches long and had sawlike edges. They must have belonged to a giant meat-eating dinosaur.

It all made sense! A big plant-eater like *Triceratops* must have had a huge meat-eating enemy. Osborn believed that these teeth were a clue. They were a hair-raising, spine-tingling peek at what *Triceratops*'s worst nightmare must have looked like. What a triumph it would be to find the whole skeleton for the museum!

4

On the Trail of a
Monster Meat-Eater

Osborn asked Brown if he could find more of the mystery meat-eater. Brown said the quarry in Wyoming seemed to be empty. He didn't think he would find any more bones there.

But those awful teeth made him think about one of his childhood heroes. Hadn't Ferdinand Hayden found teeth like these? That was fifty years ago. Hayden was a famous scientist. He had hiked alone through the badlands of Montana, study- ing the rocks.

Brown read Hayden's journal. Hayden wrote about a maze of deep canyons. He said those canyons looked something like the well-known badlands of South Dakota. Brown could picture it. He had spent many hot summer days looking for fossils in South Dakota while he was a student.

The South Dakota badlands were *bad*, Hayden said. But the Montana badlands were *worse*. High cliff walls towered all around him. The walls were made up of layers of rock. In the summer sun, those layers seemed to glow in stripes of pink and tan and blue.

Before long, Hayden said, an eerie feel- ing came over him. It was as if he were standing in a vast ancient graveyard. In the rocks were bits of bone and the teeth of strange beasts. Only later did he know. Those teeth were dinosaur teeth. They were the very first fossils in America to be identified as real dinosaur fossils.

Osborn had a lot of questions. What if the teeth in the jaw Brown found were the same as the ones Hayden had found? That would be amazing! Fossil hunters had searched the rocky cliffs for over fifty years. They always hoped to find more of Hayden's meat-eating dinosaur. They wondered what it looked like. The only other clues so far were parts of two big skulls. They were found in Canada in 1884.

Osborn pulled a book of scientific papers down from his shelf. One of the papers described the teeth. It even had

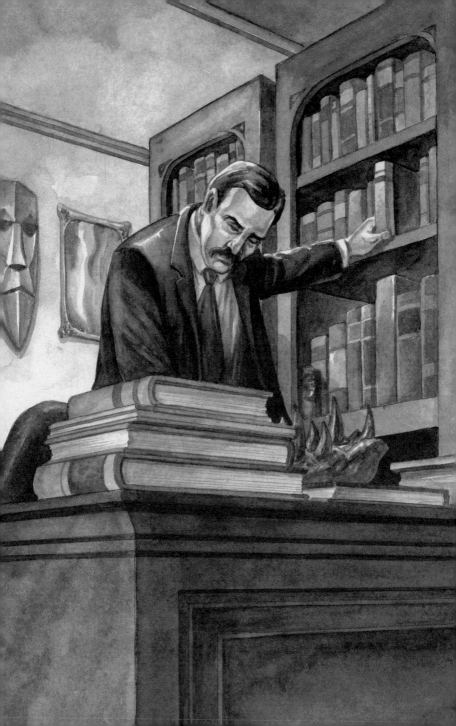

beautiful drawings of them. The teeth were named *Deinodon horridus*. In Greek, *deinos* means "terrible." *Odon* means "tooth." And *horrid?* Well, everyone knows what *that* means!

Those teeth were huge. People tried to imagine the monster that had used them. It must have been bigger than any meat-eating dinosaur anyone had ever seen.

Osborn and Brown looked at the *Deinodon* teeth. They studied the teeth in the new jaw. They were very similar. But the new teeth were bigger and thicker. Had Brown found a jaw and neck bones from "Old *Deinodon*"? Or could they be from an even bigger dinosaur? Osborn wanted more. More teeth! And more bones!

Brown had found the meat-eater's jaw in a *Triceratops* quarry. That was an important clue. *Triceratops* bones were pretty common. There are more fossil bones of plant-eating animals than there are of meat-eaters. Meat-eaters are rare. This is true with living animals, too. In any area, there are usually more plant-eating animals than hunters.

All *Triceratops* fossils are in layers of rock laid down near the end of the Age of Dinosaurs. The new jaw was in the same layers as *Triceratops*. So Brown and Osborn knew the big meat-eater lived at the same time. Osborn said if they were going to find the mystery meat-eater, they should look for *Triceratops*.

He decided to move their *Triceratops* hunt to Montana. He asked Brown to search for rock layers of the right age. Then, with a little luck, maybe the fossil hunters would find the dinosaur that had hunted *Triceratops* long, long ago.

Brown was thrilled to go back to Montana. His father had gone there often. He hauled supplies between frontier outposts. When Barnum was sixteen, his father brought him along to help. They hitched up their horse and wagon. They rode across the state. They camped under the stars at night. On that trip, Barnum fell in love with the wild Montana landscape.

He thought of those wide-open spaces. Where would he begin? Brown looked through Cope's, Marsh's, and Hayden's old notes. He studied the drawings and maps. One way or another, he'd figure it out. He was hot on the trail of the biggest meat-eating dinosaur that ever lived.

Of course, that part of their quest was

a secret! Osborn and Brown wanted to find the meat-eating dinosaur for their museum. But it wasn't long before the director of the Carnegie Museum heard about the new jaw. Osborn knew Carnegie was already looking for a *Triceratops*, too. What if Carnegie's crew found the big meat-eater first?

Once again, the two museums were in a race. Osborn wanted to win. He alerted all his workers and friends who were going out west. Everyone had to be on the lookout for any sign of *Triceratops*!

5

The Treasure Map

William Hornaday was the director of New York's Bronx Zoo. He didn't know much about fossils. He looked for living animals, not dead ones. In time, Hornaday became famous for saving the American bison. Without him, bison would surely have died out, just like the dinosaurs.

Hornaday's work took him to Montana

many times. Over the years, he got to know some of the ranchers there. And he enjoyed hunting in the wild and rugged canyons.

Henry Fairfield Osborn and William Hornaday were friends. So while Hornaday studied the animals of the West, he kept an eye out for fossils, too. In 1901, he was in Montana with a well-known Wild West photographer. One of their friends had a ranch on the banks of Hell Creek.

The men were out hunting one day when the rancher spotted three large chunks of fossil bone. Hornaday could tell that the chunks fit together. He wasn't an expert. Still, he thought they looked like a *Triceratops*'s horn. The photographer took pictures of the area where they found the fossils. As soon as he got home, Hornaday told Osborn the good news.

Osborn asked Hornaday to get in touch with Barnum Brown. Hornaday showed Brown the photos. Brown thought the rock layers looked a lot like the ones in Wyoming where he had found the jaw and the *Triceratops* bones. Were they from the same age? Brown thought so, but he would have to see them in person to be sure.

Hornaday drew Brown a map. He showed him how to get to the log cabin where the rancher lived. It was twelve miles up Hell Creek from the Missouri River. On the map, he marked the "rugged bad lands" and the "very rugged bad lands." He noted the "beautiful rolling grass uplands," the "big sagebrush flats," and the "awful ravines."

Three miles from the cabin was the east fork of Hell Creek. There, between two tall, flat-topped hills, Hornaday promised that Brown would find the treasure he was looking for.

Brown couldn't wait to get started! By May 1902, he was ready to head west. He took the train from New York City to Miles City, Montana. In Miles City, Brown met up with two co-workers. One was another scientist. The other was a camp cook.

After they left the train, all modern travel ended. For five days, they rode north on horseback. They covered 130 miles, through wide, rolling grasslands. Along the way, they shot antelope for food. Each evening, they cooked over a campfire. They gazed up at the stars at night.

By the sixth day, the grasslands were behind them. They rode to a high point of land. From there they looked out over the badlands ahead.

Across the area were many small creeks. Most of the time, the creeks were dry. But over millions of years, each small stream had cut its own canyon into the land. Many of the canyons were more than 200 feet deep. They formed a maze in the landscape.

The walls of the canyons were dazzling in the light of the sun. The rock layers made stripes of yellow, gray, green, pink, purple, brown, and blue. Brown rode through the canyons and found the layers shown in the photos. His guess had been correct. Those layers were formed near the end of the Age of Dinosaurs. They were from the time of *Triceratops*! Brown knew he had come to the right place.

After seeing the area for the first time, he wrote to a friend: "These are certainly bad lands, almost impossible lands I might say." The canyon made by Hell Creek was sizzling hot and as dry as dust. Rattlesnakes rested in the shade of every juniper bush. It was no wonder they called it Hell Creek. But as much as Brown joked about it, to him this land was heaven. It was perfect dinosaur-hunting country!

The day after they got to the log cabin, they followed Hornaday's treasure map. He had drawn a small circle between two hills. Beside the circle, he had printed neatly, "Triceratops <u>about</u> here." That's where Brown and his crew set up their tents.

They walked along the ridges and in the deep gullies. They moved slowly. Their backs were bent low. Their heads were down. They scanned every square inch of ground. A tiny piece of fossil bone could be the clue that led them to a giant.

Fossil hunters can spend days like that without finding a thing. Not this time! Hornaday's map was good. That very day, Brown spotted the *Triceratops* bones. Brown knew Osborn would be happy.

But would their *Triceratops* lead them to the mysterious hunter? Nobody could say. Brown figured he'd have to spend a while searching. But it didn't take much time at all! Before the cook called them for dinner that evening, Brown came across something very interesting.

At his feet, he found large, rounded

stones. Several had pieces of bone in them. He could tell they had tumbled down the hillside. He traced where the bits of bone had come from. Way up on the side of the rocky slope, he saw large bones sticking

out of the sand. He brushed the soft sand away to get a better look. Soon he hit hard rock.

In the rock were the bones of a huge meat-eating dinosaur. Those bones lay just as they had when the animal died, millions of years ago. Brown had been hunting dinosaurs for years. He told Osborn he "had never seen anything like it." It was "the find of the season!"

Could this be the beast with "Old *Deinodon*" teeth? Brown couldn't tell. He'd have to get the bones out of the rock first. Maybe deep in the rock he would find jaws.

6

Digging Up the Giant

Finding a dinosaur can be hard. But taking one out of the ground is the real challenge. There was so much to be done! The moment Brown laid eyes on the big bones, he began to worry. How would he ever get them out without breaking them?

At first, all he could see were parts of a few bones. They were the color of milky coffee. And they were seventy-five feet up on the side of the hill. Even worse, Brown complained, "Each bone is surrounded by the hardest blue sandstone I ever tried to work."

This was going to take time!

Brown had the tools for chipping away the rock. He had picks, chisels, rock hammers, and awls. But he needed paper, burlap, and plaster to make hard jackets. The jackets would protect the fossils once they were out of the ground. The crew would also need food for the weeks ahead. They would have to pick up supplies in the nearby town of Jordan.

As long as they were camping in the wild, Brown and his crew knew how to stay safe. They knew what to do about rattlesnakes, falling rocks, and quicksand.

Going to Jordan was a different kind of adventure.

Jordan was a small town. It was only three log cabins in a grove of cottonwood trees. It had a general store and a post office. Next to the general store was a saloon. When there was trouble in town, most of the time it started there, at the saloon.

Barnum Brown was a bit of a city slicker in the way he dressed. Even in the field, he'd sometimes wear a tie, a dressy top-coat, and shiny shoes. But Jordan was a rough-and-tumble kind of place. Some of the cowboys in town couldn't resist picking on the fancy Eastern dudes. They liked to tease them and call them "bug hunters."

"Among the cowboys," Brown wrote

in his notebook, "anyone who collected butterflies, insects of any kind . . . or fossils was a bug hunter."

One afternoon, Brown sent one of his co-workers to town to pick up their mail. The storekeeper saw a bunch of rowdy cowboys spill out of the saloon. He told the scientist to keep his head down and sneak out of town, fast.

The scientist climbed on the wagon and quietly got the horses going. He had almost made it up the hill, out of sight. Then the cowboys saw that he was getting away. They grabbed their rifles and began shooting. Lead bullets whizzed over the scientist's head!

He drove the horses to a gallop. Behind him, he heard the cowboys whooping and hollering.

Brown and his crew went to town as seldom as possible after that!

It didn't matter. The rocks kept them busy. As hard as they worked, the rocks that held the bones would barely budge. At last, Brown decided he would have to "shoot the bank." That didn't mean they would shoot the hillside with their rifles. It meant they needed to use explosives. They placed sticks of dynamite carefully in the layers of rock above the bones. Then— KABOOM! They set off the dynamite and blasted the heavy rock away.

Even with explosives, the work went slowly. By late September, the season was almost over. Fall and winter snowstorms would be coming soon. Brown had to hurry. It was time to pack up the fossils. The bones would have to withstand a long,

hard journey to the museum. Everything had to be done perfectly.

Brown was an expert fossil packer. He and his crew first wrapped each fossil in paper. Then they soaked strips of burlap in wet plaster. Quickly, before the plaster set, they wound the goopy strips around the fossil. The paper kept the plaster from sticking to the bones. When the plaster dried, the burlap strips made a hard jacket around the fossil.

For each really huge bone, they dug down into the rock all around it. They covered the top part of the bone with wet plaster strips. Then they dug tunnels under the bone. They pushed more wet plaster strips through the tunnels. When that plaster was hard, they turned the big block of bone upside down. They added plaster strips to the bottom.

When they were done, the fossil was held safely in a big white plaster case.

This took a lot of plaster! When they ran out, they mixed up flour and water instead. Brown was always neat and tidy. If anyone spattered white goop on Brown's nice shoes, he was in big trouble.

In September, they jacketed 15,000 pounds of fossils. The largest were some of the bones of the big meat-eater. Coated in plaster, the lower part of the pelvis (or hip bones) weighed 4,150 pounds. That's as heavy as a midsize car!

Besides most of the pelvis, Brown's crew had also found part of a thighbone, five bones from the back, and part of a skull bone. Along with these bones was something mysterious—a very small upper-arm bone. Brown couldn't believe this tiny arm

belonged to the big meat-eater. But he had found it, right with the other bones. It was puzzling.

The jacketed bones were packed in boxes. Then they were hauled down the bumpy road to Miles City in carts with

teams of four horses. It took eight days to cover the 130 miles.

That October, Brown stored twenty-one boxes of fossils in a warehouse in Miles City. He hired a local lumberman to watch over them. They would be safe while Brown went out looking again. He wanted to find more fossils before the really bad weather set in.

On his search, he ran into someone from the Carnegie Museum. Their crew had been digging in Montana, too. But they had not been hanging around Miles City. They knew nothing of Brown's meat-eater.

Osborn ordered a special freight-train car to come from Seattle. At Miles City, the lumberman and his workers loaded the boxes aboard.

When the fossils got to New York,

Osborn helped take off their plaster jackets. The minute he laid eyes on those bones, he knew. This meat-eater was not just the find of the season. It was the find of a lifetime!

Osborn made everyone promise to keep quiet about the skeleton. He joked in a letter about "our friends in other Museums." He did not mention any names. They knew what museum he was talking about. Above all, no one was to say a word about where the bones had been found.

7

Naming the Beast

In November 1902, Brown returned to New York. He put a crew to work cleaning the dinosaur bones. It was slow going. All the sand and bits of rock had to be carefully chipped and brushed away.

Finally Osborn and Brown had a chance to study the cleaned bones. Then they felt sure. Their new meat-eater was big enough to be Hayden's "Old *Deinodon*." In fact, like the dinosaur whose jaw Brown had found in Wyoming, it was probably even bigger. Still, Brown needed to find this animal's teeth and jaws before they could prove it.

Osborn had a lot of questions. Could more bones of the big meat-eater still be in the ground? Was more of the skull hiding in that hard blue sandstone? Brown's answer was yes!

He was eager to get back to Hell Creek to dig even deeper. But for a while, trips to other places kept him away. Finally, in 1905, Brown returned to the quarry. Osborn heard that a Carnegie crew would be working in Montana that summer, too. He was worried. Only the year before, that crew had dug up a *Triceratops* near Hell Creek. They were dangerously close to Brown's secret quarry!

Osborn hoped the Carnegie folks wouldn't stumble across the grave of the big meat-eater. His own crew was trying to get there quickly, but they almost didn't make it at all. It wasn't rattlesnakes or falling rocks or quicksand that held them up. It was a brand-new kind of problem.

In Billings, Montana, Brown bought a wagon and a team of two horses. His wife, Marion Brown, and another young scientist were with him. They loaded up their supplies and started out toward Jordan.

The horses, Dick and Blue, were strong and spirited. Every time Brown tied up Dick at night, he broke free. Then the horse raided the oat bags in the wagon. Brown had to bring the bags into his tent at night to guard them. Each morning, he and Marion woke to see Dick peering at

them through the tent flap. The horse whinnied for his meal.

The crew and horses were having fun. They were making good time, too. But one rainy day, a motorcycle roared past them on the muddy road. Motorcycles were new back then. Even in the cities, most people didn't own cars or motorcycles yet. Blue reared up in fear. He yanked free of the wagon and ran into a barbed-wire fence. The poor horse was badly hurt. There was no way he could go on pulling.

Brown sewed up Blue's wounds. Then he rode Dick all the way back to Billings. He had no other choice. It took him three days, in the hard rain and sloppy mud. He bought another horse and returned to where the crew was camped. Blue would be better in a few weeks. But the whole mishap had added a month to their trip.

Finally they made it to the ranch at Hell Creek. The rancher told Brown that the Carnegie crew had been snooping around. They had come back to search for more of the *Triceratops* they found the year before.

Brown hurried to the quarry. Happily, everything was just as they had left it. Brown told Osborn that he didn't have to worry. Their secret was safe. The rancher was pretty sure the other crew had left empty-handed.

Still, it kept raining. Brown couldn't help laughing. For once the hard rock was helping them. At least they wouldn't be getting splashed with mud.

It wasn't long before they came across the upper part of the meat-eater's pelvis. Then they found another piece of skull. Brown was very excited. He decided to make the quarry wider and deeper. He couldn't wait for extra-strong steel chisels to be sent from New York. Instead, he borrowed tools from the local ranchers.

But the sandstone was too hard even for the toughest tools. He went to Jordan to buy more dynamite. After blasting, he

hitched up the horses to a heavy metal scraper, and they dragged away the rubble.

By July 15, the quarry was a huge pit, blasted and carved out of the high cliff-side. The rock walls reflected the heat of the sun. Digging in the quarry, the crew

felt as if they were baking in an oven. "This is a heavy piece of work," Brown wrote to Osborn. "But these bones are so rare that it is worth the work."

Osborn wrote back that they should collect every single bone from the quarry. Brown and his crew chipped away at the rocks for several more weeks.

They found another huge thighbone and some ribs. Then . . . half hidden in that blue rock . . . it looked like . . . Could it be? Yes! Jawbones! This was exactly what Brown had been hoping for.

In the meantime, Osborn heard a rumor. Someone told him that the crew from the Carnegie hadn't exactly gone home empty-handed. They had found the jaws of a meat-eating dinosaur, too! Osborn knew he would have to work fast.

He wrote a description of all the bones Brown had already sent home.

In 1905, Osborn published an important scientific paper about meat-eating dinosaurs. In that paper, he named their new meat-eater. He called it *Tyrannosaurus rex*. That's Latin for "tyrant lizard king." The name captured the imagination of the world.

Still, Osborn had questions. What about the animal's arms? How could they be so tiny?

Also, the jaws and teeth were still locked in the blue rock. Had they found the dinosaur with the *Deinodon* teeth? Did their *T. rex* have even bigger teeth? The new jaws held the answer.

Those all-important jaws! It took almost a year for the museum's workers to get them free of the rock. Lucky for the American Museum of Natural History, it took the Carnegie's workers even longer to free theirs.

After the teeth and jaws had been cleaned, Osborn and Brown were thrilled. Their new meat-eater, *Tyrannosaurus rex,* was certainly related to Hayden's "Old *Deinodon*." But *T. rex*'s teeth were much bigger. Just like the teeth in Brown's Wyoming jaw, they were six inches long and as thick as bananas!

Brown had found his mystery monster. This was the terrifying hunter that could take down *Triceratops*. Without a doubt, it was the biggest meat-eating dinosaur that had ever lived. And the American Museum of Natural History was the first museum to find it!

8

The World's Greatest Dinosaur Hunter

After he dug up his first *T. rex*, Barnum Brown went back to Montana as often as he could. He searched the canyons for more dinosaurs.

Then, in the summer of 1908, he made another big find. He was walking in a canyon made by one of the little branches of the river called the Big Dry. Suddenly he spotted four tail bones. They were in the side of a sandstone hill. He dug them out. One bone led to another. Soon he had fifteen tail bones all in a row. These bones looked very familiar. He was sure they came from another *T. rex*.

Brown looked at the huge hill. Were more bones in there? If so, they were hidden under a lot of rock. Brown sighed and wiped his sweaty brow with a fine silk handkerchief. This was going to take a lot of dynamite.

Back in New York, Osborn had no problems with that. Hang the expense! All the supplies Brown needed were shipped to Jordan.

By now the cowboys in the area were very interested in what was going on. Brown had come to respect the Montana ranchers he met. A few became his lifelong friends. Nobody teased the fancy Eastern dudes anymore. The cowboys knew the scientists were not "bug hunting." They were hunting for bigger animals than any of them had ever seen.

Brown and his crew followed the tail bones into the hillside. It took lots of dynamite, a sturdy plow, and days of hard labor with picks, awls, and brushes. At the end of the tail, they found the pelvis. They kept digging—farther and farther into the tough rock. And they kept finding more bones.

But it wasn't all work. Every once in a while, they took time to relax. On the Fourth of July, one of the local ranchers hosted a big celebration. People came from miles around. After a feast of "chicken, all kinds of cake, salad and ice cream and

lemonade," everyone began to dance. That day the music and the fireworks were as loud as Barnum Brown's dynamite. Brown and his crew were the hit of the party. *T. rex*—the world's greatest dinosaur—was *America's* dinosaur!

The party went on all night and into the next day. Then, on July 6, the crew rode back to the site, bright and early. After a few more days of blasting and digging, they found the treasure of treasures. The trail of bones led to the monster's skull. This time it wasn't just part of the animal's skull. The whole thing was right there in the rock!

T. rex's head was scarier than anyone had imagined. It was almost five feet long. Its mouth was full of those long, thick, saw-edged teeth. Its powerful jaws were wide enough to swallow a whole cow in one bite.

As soon as the news reached New York, Osborn and the museum staff celebrated, too. But Osborn asked everyone to keep quiet about it until the skeleton was safely home.

Getting that beast to the museum was going to be a huge challenge. The block of stone that held the skull weighed nearly 3,000 pounds. The lower jaw was in another block. That one weighed 1,000 pounds. It took the whole summer to get the bones out of the ground.

In the fall, the snow and wind started again. Brown's crew had to get the fossils out of the quarry soon. They wrapped the bones in plaster jackets. Brown built big wooden crates to hold them.

The quarry was in the middle of nowhere. The nearest road was miles away. They loaded as many crates on their wagon as it would hold. The horses pulled the heavy wagon over the rough land. Soon icy rain began to fall. The ground became soft. Before they knew it, the wagon was stuck. Brown had to ride into town and bring back more horses to help.

After several trips, all the crates were finally at the main road. Brown and his crew loaded up five wagons. What a grand parade it must have been! Sixteen horses pulled the wagons north, forty-

five miles to the train station in Glasgow, Montana. There the treasure was put into a railcar. On October 12, 1908, the most complete *T. rex* ever found rolled into New York City.

Finally the new *T. rex* was safe and sound at the museum. Osborn couldn't wait to tell the news to the world. Brown had found an "absolutely perfect skull!"

By then everyone knew that Brown's big Wyoming jaw—the one that started the whole hunt—was also from a *T. rex*. To find one *Tyrannosaurus rex* is amazing. To find three is something only one person in the world has ever done. That person is Barnum Brown. Fossil fans declared him the world's greatest dinosaur hunter. Instead of "Mr. Brown," kids began calling him "Mr. Bones."

President Jesup was able to retire happy. His beloved museum was healthy and growing. Money poured in. Artists painted backdrops for beautiful displays. And young fossil hunters planned more trips. There was no doubt about it. Albert Bickmore's dream was coming true. The American Museum of Natural History would soon be among the biggest and best museums in the world.

9

The World Goes Wild for *T. rex*

Osborn was happy but over-whelmed. Now the museum had not one but two *T. rex* skeletons to put on display. He made plans to add another new wing to the museum. None of the museum's great halls was big enough for both gigantic newcomers.

Each *T. rex* was over forty-five feet long. That's longer than a school bus! The skeletons would stand eighteen to twenty feet high. Next to a *T. rex,* a grown man would reach no higher than the monster's knee.

What about that little bitty arm bone, though? Osborn studied all the *T. rex* bones more closely. Strange as it seemed, that small arm bone did belong to the giant. Why were its arms so small? Osborn wasn't sure. But they are the one and only feature about a *T. rex* that is not super-sized and super-scary.

Osborn wondered how the dinosaurs should stand. He asked an artist to make two small copies of every bone in a *T. rex* skeleton. Then the miniature bones could be put together. The little models could be used to try out different poses.

Osborn called on his old friend at the

Bronx Zoo, William Hornaday. Someone who studied living animals would be good at finding the most lifelike poses for their extinct giants. Hornaday sent him to the zoo's reptile expert, Raymond Ditmars.

Ditmars came up with a vivid scene. The two *T. rex*es would be fighting each other over a meal. A duckbill dinosaur would lie dead between them. Museum visitors could ask themselves, "Which *T. rex* will get the prize?" It would be anyone's guess. The two monsters would be stopped in action. Each was forever ready to lunge at the other!

Everyone agreed on the poses. Then the huge bones of one skeleton were mounted on a heavy steel framework. To get just one dinosaur up took seven years. The crew started with the skeleton Brown found in

1908. No legs or feet had been found with that *T. rex*. The 1902 *T. rex* did have those bones. So casts were made from them. The feet had to be placed closer together than Ditmars first suggested. Otherwise the monster might fall over!

The skull was the biggest problem of all. It was way too heavy. How could they get it on the framework? No one could figure it out. They had to mount a plaster cast of it instead.

In 1915, *T. rex* was finally ready to be shown to the world. There wasn't enough room to fit it in the museum's Dinosaur Hall. Osborn was forced to squeeze it into the Hall of the Age of Man.

The display was dazzling. The deadly-looking beast loomed over museum visitors. The artist's models, in their dramatic poses, went on exhibit along with the one full-size skeleton.

Soon *Tyrannosaurus rex* was headline news. Reporters raved about the scary-toothed giant who terrorized the West. It was a beast that could "easily make a meal of an elephant!"

"No!" Osborn told them. "Dinosaurs did not live at the same time as human beings or elephants!"

Osborn wanted to hurry up and get the Tyrant Lizard King in the hall "where it properly belonged." Wisely, the designers had set the skeleton on a big platform with small rollers. The dinosaur could be moved without having to take the whole thing apart. In 1917, *T. rex* was finally moved to the Dinosaur Hall. Osborn breathed a sigh of relief.

Before long, the animal became famous all over the world. Dinosaur murals, movies, ads, and toys were created. They all featured everyone's new favorite—*Tyrannosaurus rex*!

The mounted skeleton of *T. rex* had something wrong with it, though. Most kids today would spot the mistake right away. What was it? Three-fingered hands! Today kids know that all tyrannosaurs have two-fingered hands. That's one of the first ways to tell if a meat-eating dinosaur is a *T. rex*.

A very complete *Gorgosaurus*, a close *T. rex* relative, had been found in Canada. By 1914, Osborn knew what *T. rex*'s hands really looked like. The *Gorgosaurus* skeleton had very good hand bones. Who could believe it? A giant tyrannosaur's hand was

a tiny little thing with two fingers. But Osborn didn't find the time to fix *T. rex*'s hands until many years later.

It turned out that the Carnegie Museum of Natural History's meat-eating jaws were from a *T. rex*, too. But the Carnegie Museum did not find any more bones from their animal. The American Museum of Natural History was proud of its beast. For years, no other museum in the world had a whole *T. rex* skeleton.

Osborn had always planned to put up the other *T. rex* skeleton. But years went by, and the first *T. rex* stayed in the museum's basement. No one had the time or the space to display it.

In 1929, the Great Depression began. For the museum, and for everyone in the country, money was a problem again. The new wing Osborn dreamed of was not built.

10

The First *T. rex* Finds a Home

In December 1940, Barnum Brown had a talk with a friend from the Carnegie Museum of Natural History. It was time, Brown said, for the rivalry to end. People had more to worry about than the so-called bone wars.

By then the Depression was over. But World War II was under way. Bombs had hit museums in Europe. Priceless treasures were in danger of being lost every day.

If the American Museum of Natural History was bombed, the two best *T. rex* skeletons in the world could be gone in an instant. Blown to bits! It might be decades before anyone found another *T. rex*. For safety, Brown and the directors decided to sell the first *T. rex* to the Carnegie Museum.

Down in the basement of the American Museum of Natural History, workers labeled each bone. They dipped strips of burlap in flour paste and made new jackets for the bones. At last, the bones were ready for shipping. They filled fifteen wooden crates and four cardboard boxes.

A big truck eased under a small walking bridge between two of the museum's main wings. It pulled into the narrow parking area and stopped at the shipping door. Barnum Brown watched as his pride and joy was loaded on the truck. The first *T. rex* was going to its new home.

In 1942, all the bones were put together. The skeleton went on display for the first time in the Carnegie Museum's Dinosaur Hall. Visitors have come from all over the world to marvel at the great meat-eater ever since.

Barnum Brown lived to be ninety years old. Sadly, his wife, Marion, died in 1910. But he and his second wife, Lilian Brown, hunted for fossils in the American West and in many different countries. Brown was the first to find many other new dinosaurs. And he gave talks all across the United States.

Right up until a few days before he died,

he loved to lead tours of the American Museum of Natural History. He told everyone that the fossils he had found were his "children." His favorite child, of course, was *Tyrannosaurus rex*.

T. rex will always be a favorite of museum visitors, too. But Brown wanted people to remember that *T. rex* is more than just an amazing museum exhibit. He wrote exciting stories about *T. rex*es and their world. He brought dinosaurs back to life for museum visitors.

Real *T. rex*es once hunted and fought. They mated and raised their babies in this place we now call America. Their bones tell us of a time long before human life began—a time when *Tyrannosaurus rex* ruled this land!

Afterword

Barnum Brown's 1908 *T. rex* is still at the American Museum of Natural History in New York City. If you want to see the first *T. rex*—the one Brown discovered in 1902—it's standing in the Carnegie Museum of Natural History in Pittsburgh.

Tyrannosaurus rex is the biggest member of the tyrannosaur family. We now know that the parts of skulls found in Canada in 1884 are from a smaller tyrannosaur called *Albertosaurus*. Hayden's famous *Deinodon* teeth probably belong to *Gorgosaurus*. *Alioramus, Daspletosaurus,* and *Tarbosaurus* are a few other types of tyrannosaurs.

Over the years, scientists have learned more about how tyrannosaurs may have walked, run, and stood. *T. rex*'s neck and tail balance like a seesaw over its powerful hind legs. Today both of Brown's *T. rex*es have new poses. They are no longer rearing up with tails down. Now they lean forward. They look as if they are stalking their prey.

After Brown's finds in the early 1900s, no one found another *T. rex* in the United States until the late 1960s. Today parts of

more than thirty-five *T. rex* skeletons have been found. Those fossils are at museums in the United States, Canada, and Great Britain.

So far, there are only two *T. rex* skeletons

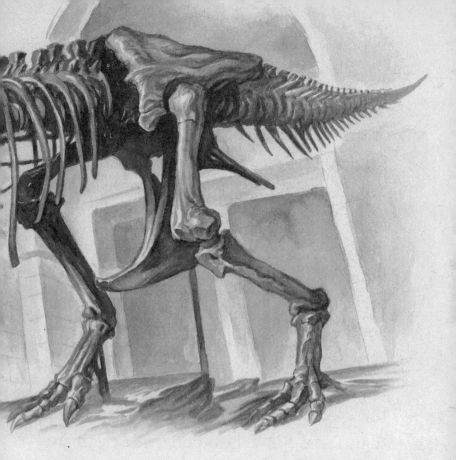

bigger and more complete than the one Brown found in 1908. They are nicknamed "Sue" and "Stan." Both were dug up by crews led by Peter Larson of the Black Hills Institute of Geological Research in Hill City,

South Dakota. Sue was found in 1990 by Susan Hendrickson. You can see that *T. rex* at the Field Museum in Chicago. Stan was found in 1992 by Stan Sacrison. Stan is on display at the Black Hills Institute.

Is *T. rex* still considered the biggest meat-eating land animal that ever lived? Bones of a huge meat-eating dinosaur called *Giganotosaurus* were discovered in South America in 1994. That dinosaur is very similar to the great African meat-eater *Carcharodontosaurus*. The biggest of these beasts are a little longer and taller than *T. rex*. But *T. rex*'s bones and teeth are heftier. And *T. rex*'s head is much wider. On average, *T. rex*es probably weighed more and had more powerful meat-chomping jaws than their African and South American cousins.

Acknowledgments

A very special thanks to Dr. William Clemens for introducing me to William Hornaday's treasure map and for lending me The Log Book of the Bug Hunters. Thanks also to Dr. Lowell Dingus and Susan K. Bell for helping me uncover hard-to-find facts about Barnum Brown's life and the history of the AMNH. Most of all, thanks to Dr. Robert T. Bakker for his expert help at every stage.

THE STORY BEHIND THE STORY

FINDING THE FIRST

T. REX

THE MESOZOIC ERA

The Mesozoic Era is divided into three time periods—
Triassic, Jurassic, and Cretaceous.

Triassic Period (252–201 million years ago)
> 228 million years ago, the first dinosaurs appear.
> The first mammals, turtles, and reptiles appear.

Jurassic Period (201–145 million years ago)
> Sauropods appear.
> Megalosaurs and allosaurs appear.
> The first birds appear.

Cretaceous Period (145–66 million years ago)
> *T. rex* appears.
> *Alamosaurus* appears.
> *Triceratops* appears.

Dinosaurs become extinct. (65 million years ago)

THE FIRST DINOSAURS

The earth's first dinosaurs appeared in the middle of the Triassic Period, around 228 million years ago. These early dinosaurs walked on two legs and were meat-eaters. None of them were much bigger than a German shepherd.

JURASSIC GIANTS

During the Jurassic Period, between 201 and 145 million years ago, many different dinosaurs ruled the earth. The most famous are the long-necked, plant-eating dinosaurs called sauropods. They are the biggest land animals the world has ever seen—ten times heavier than elephants! Meat-eating dinosaurs, such as allosaurs and megalosaurs, hunted the giant plant-eaters. By the end of the Jurassic, most of the big sauropods and allosaurs, as well as many others, had died out in North America.

CRETACEOUS CREATURES

The first tyrannosaurs appeared late in the Cretaceous Period, about 80 million years ago. *Tyrannosaurus rex* was the tallest and most powerful tyrannosaur. *T. rex* was king of the Cretaceous! *Triceratops,* with long, sharp horns and strong limbs, was the most dangerous plant-eater in North America at that time. The long-necked *Alamosaurus* was the biggest. Then, 65 million years ago, all the giant dinosaurs died out. The end of the Age of Dinosaurs had come.

WHAT ARE FOSSILS?

When most animals and plants die, they break up and become part of the soil. But sometimes they become hard and change to stones, called fossils. Fossils can be teeth, shells and bones, or even footprints and outlines of where a body was.

Fossils can only form if the conditions are just right. First, the animal or plant gets buried in thick mud or sand, called sediment. Slowly, water and minerals in the sediment mix together and make the remains hard, like stone. This change happens over a long time . . . sometimes hundreds of millions of years!

Scientists try to look for fossils trapped in the earth, because they can show us a lot about the creatures that lived long ago. But finding fossils can be tough, like finding a needle in a haystack.

T. REX...WITH FEATHERS?!

When you see paintings of *T. rex*es, they usually look like giant scaly-skinned reptiles. But some scientists think that *T. rex*es may actually have been feathery.

The only way to know for sure would be to find a *T. rex* with fossilized feathers. So far, no one has found *T. rex* feathers. But that's not too surprising. The hard parts of an animal—bones or shells—are much more likely to get fossilized than soft parts like feathers.

More than thirty types of dinosaurs *have* been found with feathers. And almost all of them come from a group of meat-eating dinosaurs called coelurosaurs. Tyrannosaurs all belong to this group. Most feathered coelurosaurs are nowhere near the size of *T. rex*es. But in 2012, paleontologists in China found a two-ton tyrannosaur with feathers. They named it *Yutyrannus huali,* or "beautiful feathered tyrant". If *T. rex*'s close relatives—even the big ones—had feathers, then maybe *T. rex* did too.

About the Author

Kathleen Weidner Zoehfeld has written more than fifty books for young readers, including two other Stepping Stones, *Fossil Fever* and *The Curse of King Tut's Mummy*; *Wild Lives: A History of the People and Animals of the Bronx Zoo*; and *Dinosaur Parents, Dinosaur Young*, which was an ALA-ALSC Notable Children's Book.

She lives in a house surrounded by fog and trees, on a hillside overlooking San Francisco Bay. When Kathleen is not at her desk writing, you'll find her volunteering at her local museum or wandering the badlands of the Wild West in search of fossil treasures.